God is Able...

by
Elmer Towns
and
John Maxwell

Contributing Editor Douglas Porter
and Wayne Cook
Creative Editor Larry Gilbert

Ephesians Four Ministries
CHURCH GROWTH INSTITUTE
P.O. Box 7, Elkton, MD 21922-0007

1-800-553-GROW (4769)

TABLE OF CONTENTS

Dear Reader,

This book will help you to take steps of faith. As a result, you will grow in Christ. When you realize that GOD IS ABLE . . . to meet all your needs, you can grow in your faith.

This book is about stewardship. It was not prepared to motivate you to give more money to your church. It will help you realize that GOD IS ABLE... to give you more when you obey Him. When you understand God's principles of stewardship, you will prosper spiritually and financially.

These messages were preached at Skyline Church, San Diego, California, winter, 1985. The church grew in financial giving by over $10,000 per week. Over 300 people began tithing as a result of the first GOD IS ABLE... stewardship program.

As God has used the message of this book in others, may He use it in your life. May you learn the ability of God to meet your every need.

Sincerely yours in Christ,

Elmer L. Towns
Lynchburg, Virginia

John Maxwell
Atlanta, Georgia

CHAPTER ONE

STEWARDSHIP IS MANAGEMENT

BIBLE IN FOCUS: "Moreover, it is required in stewards, that a man be found faithful." (I Corinthians 4:2)

LESSON SCRIPTURE:

Hear another parable: There was a certain householder, which planted a vineyard and hedged it round about, and digged a winepress in it, and built a tower, and let it out to husbandmen, and went into afar country:

And when the time of the fruit drew near, he sent his servants to the husbandmen, that they might receive the fruits of it.

And the husbandmen took his servants, and beat one, and killed another, and stoned another.

Again, he sent other servants more than the first' and they did unto them likewise.

But last of all he sent unto them his son, saying, They will reverence my son.

But when the husbandmen saw the son, they said among themselves, This is the heir; come let us kill him, and let us seize on his inheritance.

And they caught him, and cast him out of the vineyard and slew him.

When the lord therefore of the vineyard cometh, what will he do unto those husbandmen?

They say unto him, He will miserably destroy those wicked men, and will let out his vineyard unto other husbandmen, which shall render him fruits in their seasons.

Jesus saith unto them, Did ye never read in the scriptures, The stone which the builders rejected, the same is become the head of the corner: this is the Lord's doing, and it is marvelous in our eyes?

Therefore say I unto you, The kingdom of God shall be taken from you, and given to a nation bringing forth the fruits thereof.

And whosoever shall fall on this Stone shall be broken.' but on whomsoever it shall fall it will grind him to powder.

And when the chief priests and Pharisees had heard his parables, they perceived that he spake of them.

But when they sought to lay hands on him, the), feared the multitude, because they took him for a prophet.

Matthew 21:33-46

INTRODUCTION

At her death on March 30, 1975, most people assumed Bertha Adams was just another welfare victim. An autopsy revealed she had severe malnutrition and evidences of poverty were abundant in her disheveled apartment. Lack of heat, lack of food, lack of the basic necessities of life -- there could only be one conclusion. Bertha Adams was an obvious example of one who was missed by the national safety net of social spending.

But then, while taking inventory of her personal effects, authorities found two keys. Trusting a hunch, they took the keys to a neighborhood bank and found her safety deposit box stuffed with $799,000.00 in cash. Also, crammed into that box were hundreds of valuable and negotiable stock certificates, bonds and other securities.

Bertha Adams had a stewardship problem. She viewed possessions as something to be hoarded. She did not understand that the blessings of life were given to her to be used and invested rather than to keep. Bertha Adams did not understand that the purpose of life was to manage her resources, not selfishly clutch them to her bosom.

God has given us things in this life not to hoard but to manage for His glory. One of the titles of the Christian in the New Testament is the term "steward". The Greek word *oikonomos* is a compound word derived from the term for house *(oikos)* and the verb to arrange *(nemo)*. The word *oikonomos* (steward) was a servant designated as the manager of a household, estate or other affairs of his master. The Christian is a steward of all the resources God has given us including time, talent and treasure. A good steward manages his time, talent and treasure for the glory of God. But like Bertha Adams, there are many Christians who have misunderstood stewardship and are poor managers of the resources of God under our control.

WRONG VIEWS OF STEWARDSHIP

Many mistakenly think that stewardship is fundraising. We often think that a stewardship program in a local church is raising money much as the community agencies raise money. Even though money is raised for the church budget, that should never be the bottom line. A stewardship program should teach church members how God wants us to spend our money. When we realize that all our money belongs to God, not just ten percent (the tithe), we will spend our money as stewards for God. A steward is a money-manager for God. When Christians are properly taught, we will not only give liberally to God, we will also spend our remaining funds according to God's plan. As a result, we will prosper and our church giving will continue to grow.

Stewardship is not talking people out of money. It's teaching people how to use the money properly.

We misunderstand the meaning of stewardship because the term has been misused Many of us think stewardship is giving money, rather than managing our assets for God. We can only give what we own. If we realize we do not own something in the first place, it is easier to give back to God. We do not own our money, possessions, or even the clothes on our back. Everything belongs to God.

If we drive a company car downtown, we know it is not our car. We are only using it for business. That is how we should treat our possessions. God is letting us use our money for His business. A salesman must use the company car for the purpose of the business. The company usually gives the salesman or other employee instructions, rules and limits in using its resources. God has also given us the instruction needed for using HIS time, talent and treasures delegated to us. Therefore, a stewardship program should educate church members in the use of time, talent and treasure for the Glory of God.

Many of us think possessions are permanent. We think we can keep things indefinitely. Though we all know *"we* can't take it with us", we often think we are an exception. Though the Bible teaches we leave this world as naked as we entered it (compare Job 1.21), we often think that somehow we will escape that law. Functionally, we think of things as permanent rather than temporary.

If we are confused and frustrated in our stewardship of financial resources, it may be because we see them primarily as permanent personal assets that someone is trying to take away from us. When we view stewardship as management of God's resources rather than permanent personal ownership, the "stew" is removed from "stewardship".

MANAGING YOUR TREASURES

Jesus described a landowner who found and purchased a field, tilled the soil, planted a vineyard, planted a thick hedge about the perimeter of it and dug wells to irrigate the vineyard. The vineyard was equipped with a tower which not only provided housing for the workers but also was a part of the security system designed to protect the vineyard from thieves and wild animals. He did everything to make the vineyard productive and then committed it to the workers. They were to produce a crop and pay him rent in the form of some portion of the crop. The owner then left the vineyard and went away.

The story Jesus told could have been about any one of the hundreds of vineyards scattered throughout Palestine in his day. It was common for wealthy investors to purchase and build well equipped vineyards and then rent them out to tenant farmers. Because of civil unrest in Judea, most wealthy Greek or Roman landlords preferred to live elsewhere and viewed property in Judea as an income property. Like most of the parables of Jesus, there was nothing foreign to the setting of this parable that His listeners would have had difficulty understanding.

Actually, the parable may be as much based on the Old Testament as on some local Judean setting. In the Old Testament, Israel was described as the vineyard of God (Isaiah 5:7). The context of Jesus's parable was obvious to the chief priests and Pharisees who first heard the story. They knew this simple story had a specific application to the nation of Israel and her response to the servants and Son of God. They realized Jesus was accusing them of poor stewardship as managers of Israel, the vineyard of God. In the parable, Jesus reminded the Jewish leaders of several important stewardship principles. Those principles apply as much to us today as they did to the people Jesus gave the parable to.

We are blessed with many benefits. In this parable, the landowner saw to it that the vineyard was completely equipped, lacking nothing that was necessary to run the business of the vineyard efficiently. Like every vineyard in Palestine, this one was equipped with a winepress, probably carved out of a solid rock although occasionally these were made with bricks. The tower provided housing for the workers and also served as a watchtower where a worker could sec that no one or nothing that might be unwanted had invaded the vineyard The fence around the vineyard was probably a thick thorny hedge that would discourage the wild boars which might have damaged or destroyed the vineyard and thieves who might otherwise steal the crop.

The owner expected the workers to manage the vineyard for him. We Christians are similar to the workers and God is the owner. Our stewardship is to manage the vineyard for Him. Everything in this world belongs to God, who created it and has redeemed it. He not only owns the resources in the world, but He has also given us good minds, good health, circumstances to get an education and even initiative to provide for our families. We do not own the things about us, we are not even owners of our health or desires. God has given us everything. He expects us to use them for His glory.

The Psalmist recognized the source of all his benefits and responded, "I will praise thee; for I am fearfully and wonderfully made. Marvelous are thy works, and that my soul knoweth right well" (Psalm 139:14). When we consider all that God has blessed us with, it is embarrassing to see how little we have done with it. Perhaps the greatest waste in the world is to have the potential God has given us and not do a thing with it. A good steward will manage these resources for the master's best interest.

Out of sight, out of mind. When the owner is out of our sight, he is usually out of our minds. The parable indicates that the landowner committed his vineyard to workers and "went into a far country" (Matthew 21:33). Absentee landlords were very popular in Palestine because the area had a lot of civil unrest and lacked the luxuries common in other parts of the Roman empire. In the story, this phrase describes God in Heaven.

These workers were not different from most people. When we are not around people, we tend to forget their birthdays, or things that are important to them. The longer the Owner is gone and the less we see Him, the more we forget about Him. We forget that God has given us everything. Some of us realize that God gave us families, homes, jobs and things like our cars and furniture. But after we work hard for a promotion or extra things like a spa or a computer, we eventually begin to think we have obtained those things by ourselves. The longer we see the things that God has given us without recognizing His ownership, the more likely we begin seeing them as our own. We forget that God is our owner and has allowed us all that we have.

Charles Spurgeon, during a Sunday morning offering, walked up and down the middle aisle, watching everyone putting money into the offering plates. Someone asked, "Why did you do that?" He answered very simply, "God watches you every week." Sometimes we think if we are out of God's sight, we are out of His mind. But God see everything we do with His money.

Harvest time reveals the heart. When there were no grapes on the vine, the workers did not have any problem with the owner coming and taking what was his. As a matter of fact, the workers were usually glad to have the owner visit the vineyard. But once there was fruit on the vine, the workers became very possessive of what they thought was theirs.

On many occasions partners have gone into business together and enjoyed working together until there was a profit and money on the table to be divided. The best friendships have been destroyed when there was money involved.

Many children have wept together at funerals over the loss of a parent. But when they came to divide the inheritance, their greed became evident. They would argue, fight and take one another to court. Harvest reveals the selfish hearts of people.

Often when we are poor, we let God have everything because we have nothing: But when we accumulate a few possessions, then we become very "possessive" about those possessions. Nine-tenths of nothing is still nothing; so is a tenth of nothing.

A wealthy man went to many churches telling how he gave his last twenty dollars to God and became a multi-millionaire. A lady stood in one of his meetings and asked, "Would you give your last million to God?"

There is always a crisis of stewardship when we have something. If we remember that everything belongs to God, we will have no trouble giving it back to Him.

A man placed four quarters on the kitchen counter and told the family the quarters were for the mission bank. He said, "Now, one quarter is for your mother, one for me, one for your sister, and one for you." The little boy picked up his quarter, rubbed it, and put it into his pocket. "Dad, can I have another quarter for missions?" he asked. When the little boy had nothing, he was willing to give his quarter for missions, but when he had it, it was hard to put in the bank for God's work.

If we do not tithe on ten thousand dollars a year, we will never tithe on a million dollars a year. We deceive ourselves when we say that we will give more when we have more and do not give when we have little.

God expects a return. When a Palestinian landowner chose to rent out his vineyard, he would choose one of three common lease agreements. Under the first, he could form an agreement in which the laborers received a portion of the produce as payment for their labor and the rest belonged to the landowner. A second type of agreement required a set rent to be paid. The third was by far the most common form of lease. It stipulated a certain portion of the crop was collected by the landowner in lieu of rent regardless of the nature of the harvest. The context of this parable assumes this third kind of lease was in place.

Like any investment-oriented businessman, God expects a good return on the resources He has placed under our control. Surveying the parables of Jesus, it is significant that whenever the master went on a long journey, he always came back looking for his return. God created man in His image and likeness and we mirror Him. He has given us our minds, our incentives and the opportunity to make something of our lives. God wants us to use our gifts and abilities for a good return to Him.

God's belief in us has no limits. The owner of the vineyard had the incredible belief in his employees that they would bring a return on his investment. First, he gave control over his resources. Further, he expected their full cooperation. Finally, he refused to believe his workers were in revolt against him. The owner kept sending people back to collect on his investment. The workers beat the first one, killed another and stoned the third. When additional servants were sent out by the owner, they met the same fate. The owner continued to think the best of the tenants and sent his own son whom they also killed.

THE TREATMENT OF THE SERVANTS

Matthew 21:35	Prophets	Jerusalem
1. Beating	1. Jeremiah 37:15; 38:16	
2. Killing	2. Jeremiah 26:20-23	Matthew 23:37
3. Stoning	3. II Chronicles 24:21	

Until this point in the story everything has been very credible. Here, however, the actions of the landlord were most unusual. Many commentators have observed that no person would send his son into a situation where his servants had been repeatedly abused and killed. The natural response of a landowner under such circumstances would be to send in the authorities to deal with the delinquent tenants. The contrast here is between what men would do and what God has done. God did send His Son to a nation which had consistently rejected the prophets and ultimately rejected the Son also (John 1:11). But the application goes far beyond the Jewish nation. Paul reminded a predominantly Gentile church, "But God commendeth His love toward us in that, while we were yet sinners, Christ died for us" (Romans 5:8). God loves us so much that even when we "hoard" or try to keep what belongs to Him, He continues to give us another chance.

Our accountability to God is inevitable. We are accountable to God for what He has given us. We are not accountable for what we don't have, only for what is committed to us to manage. There is coming a day when every one of us will give an account of our stewardship to God. The parable tells, "When the lord, therefore, of the vineyard cometh..." (21:40). It is significant that Jesus did not say *if he* comes, but *when* he comes. If God has given us a stewardship to manage for Him, then a day is coming when we must give an account to Him. All are accountable to God, and the day of reckoning is sure.

Ownership is always the issue. The owner of the vineyard owned the resources, but the workers thought they owned it. The issue in the parable was who owned the vineyard. For those of us who have a problem of stewardship with our money, the issue is usually not ignorance or lack of money; the issue is ownership. If any of us have a problem with stewardship in our lives today, there is one issue that has to be settled. The issue is always the same -- ownership of the vineyard. If we realize that God owns all our money, then there will be no problem with giving back what is His. In the parable, the master had to settle the issue. He had to come and take the vineyard from his workers.

The vineyard belonged to the owner. Just because the owner allowed someone else to work in his vineyard, it did not mean it belonged to the worker. Though the workers may have developed an emotional attachment to the vines and the vineyard, it still did not belong to them. The problem with the workers in this parable was they were treating the vineyard as their own and when the opportunity to settle the ownership issue by killing the heir was available to them, they did not hesitate in their attempt to "seize on his inheritance" (21:38).

A good steward understands who owns his possessions and recognizes his role not as one who possesses something, but one who passes it on. When he understands that his possessions are not his own, then he can become a good manager of what God has given to him. We are simply a manager of the blessings that God has given to us. It is our duty to pass them on to other people.

Judgment is based on stewardship. The landowner's treatment of the tenants was directly related to their treatment of his servants and son. When Jesus asked His listeners how they thought the landowner would respond to the death of his son, they responded, "He will miserably destroy those wicked men" (21:41). In recording that statement, Matthew used the expression *kakous kakos,* an emphatic alliteration not easily translated into English. The intent of the statement is to show a relationship between the character of the tenants and their well deserved treatment by the landowner. The following chart includes several attempts to translate the spirit of this statement into the English language.

KAKOUS KAKOS (MATTHEW 21:41)

He will miserably destroy those miserable men.
He will bring those bad men to a bad end.
He will badly destroy those bad men.
He will bring these evil men to an evil end.
Those wretches he will put to a wretched death.
He will bring those wretches to a wretched end.
Miserable men! Miserably will he destroy them.
Bemuse they are evil, he will bring an evil destruction upon them.

The landowner judged the workers based on their stewardship (management). They were not judged for what they did not have but what they had done with what they were given. Some of us sit in a pew and think God does not need our possessions. That is not the issue. Others of us think we need to give to God because He only has enough gas to get Him through today and He needs our help for tomorrow. Still others of us think we will give to God because it will help us when we come into judgment. Do we think it will keep God from being angry with us? These are no the reasons to give to God. He owns our resources and we manage them for Him. We give back to Him what is His.

First, we need to settle the issue of ownership. Does God own us and our lives? Secondly, we need to settle the issue of trust. Are we going to trust our money, or are we going to put our trust in God? When we have difficulty with stewardship we actually have difficulty trusting God..

We lose eventually what we keep selfishly. The tenant farmers who were apparently motivated in their actions by the overwhelming desire to hold on to that which was not theirs to .keep, were at the end of this account completely divorced from the vineyard. Jesus applied the parable to the Jewish nation noting, "Therefore say I unto you, The kingdom of God shall be taken from you and given to a nation bringing forth the fruits of it" (21:43). That which the nation attempted to hoard for themselves was given to a nation which could be entrusted as worthy stewards.

Jim Elliott, a missionary martyred in South America by a primitive tribe he sought to reach with the gospel, once observed, "He is no fool who gives what he cannot keep, to gain what he cannot lose." What we keep selfishly for ourselves we eventually lose. Bertha Adams had the. keys to a safety deposit box crammed full of cash and negotiable securities, but she still died of malnutrition. Because she tried to hang on to what she had rather than using it for the enrichment of her life, she lived the life of a beggar. She did not know how to Use her money.

The closer we are to God, the more giving we are of ourselves. When we understand the context and immediate application of this parable, we begin to gain an insight into the very character of God. Jesus was the Son that the Father was sending to stewards who had repeatedly abused the servants. Still, God was giving long after most landowners would have called the authorities. But giving is a natural response coming from God's heart of love. While we may be able to give without loving, it is impossible to love without giving. "For God so *loved* the world that He *gave...*" (John 3:16). When we begin to love as God loves, we will want to give as God gave. In contrast, the farther we draw away from God, the more stingy we will become with our assets and energies.

CONCLUSION

Different people will respond to biblical principles of stewardship in different ways. Sometimes, as the Holy Spirit convicts us of our shortcomings in this area, we, like the chief priests and Pharisees, are inclined to get upset or angry. When that happens, we must be careful to deal with the problem before it turns into the poison of bitterness. If we were injured and cut, we would be aware of the pain associated with the wound. We would wonder about the wisdom of a doctor who inflicts more pain on the already sore area by applying iodine to the wound. But the pain we would experience would be part of the healing process. Without the iodine, we would run the risk of infection.

The following chart outlines healthy and unhealthy attitudes of stewardship. As you examine it, take time to make personal application even if it feels somewhat uncomfortable to do so. Allow it to diagnose and begin treating any unhealthy attitude you might have in the area of stewardship. Don't allow the discomfort of treating a minor ailment result in allowing that ailment to develop into a major infection.

I am Manager	I am Owner
I am Thankful	I am Proud
Master's Kingdom	My Kingdom
Things are Transient	Things are Permanent
I want to please others	I want to please myself

We can begin removing the "stew" from stewardship today. It all begins when we recognize ourselves as the stewards or managers of the various resources God has chosen to entrust to us. Only when we see Him as the owner of all things can we begin to understand our relationship to God as stewards. That also settles the giving issue in our life. As Oswald J. Smith observed, "Not how much of *my* money will I give to God, but how much of God's money will I keep for myself?"

CHAPTER TWO

STEWARDSHIP IS RESPONSIBILITY

BIBLE IN FOCUS: "So, then, everyone of us shall give account of himself to God." (Romans 14:12)

LESSON SCRIPTURE:

And as they heard these things, he added, and spoke a parable, because he was near to Jerusalem, and because they though that the kingdom of God should immediately appear.

He said, therefore, A certain nobleman went into a far country to receive for himself a kingdom, and to return.

And he called his ten servants, and delivered them ten pounds, and said unto them, Occupy till I come.

But his citizens hated him, and sent a message after him, saying, We will not have this man to reign over as.

And it came to pass that, when he was returned, having received the kingdom, then he commanded these servants to be called unto him, to whom he had given the money, that he might know how much every man had gained by trading.

Then came the first, saying, Lord, thy pound hath gained ten pounds.

And he said unto him, Well, thou good servant; because thou hast been faithful in a very little, have thou authority over ten cities.

And the second came, saying, Lord, thy pound hath gained five pounds.

And he said to him also, Be thou also over five cities.

And another came, saying, Lord, behold, here is thy pound, which I have kept laid up in a napkin;

For I feared thee, because thou art an austere man; thou takest up that thou layedst not down, and reapest that thou didst not sow.

And he saith unto him, Out of thine own mouth will I judge thee, thou wicked servant. Thou knewest that I was an austere man, taking up that I laid not down, and reaping that I did not sow.

Why, then, gavest not thou my money into the bank, that at my coming I might have required mine own with interest?

And he said unto them that stood by, Take from him the pound, and give it to him that hath ten pounds.

(And they said unto him, Lord, he hath ten pounds.)

For I say unto you, Unto everyone who hath shall be given; and from

him that hath not, even that which he hath shall be taken away from him.
But those mine enemies, who would not that I should reign over
them, bring here, and slay them before me.

Luke 19:11-27

INTRODUCTION

An advertising slogan' in a well-known television commercial challenges the viewer, "Be all you can be!" Similarly, a leading Christian
university challenges prospective students with the statement, "Be all
God meant you to be." Although these catchy maxims are not biblical
texts, they certainly express a biblical truth. God expects each of us to
develop all of our potential to the glory of God. mediocrity always falls
short of God's perfect will for our lives.

Jesus told several parables emphasizing this very principle. Just before
coming to Jerusalem to die for the sins of the world, he told the story
which is the basis of this study (Luke 19:11-27). Later in the city, he
repeated a similar story emphasizing several similar principles (Matthew
25:14-30). While these stories were different, even a casual reading of
both of them will reveal several similarities. In both cases, a master
entrusted his riches to his servants while he was occupied away from his
estate. In both cases, they were servants with some degree of success in
investing their master's wealth and turning a profit. And both stories
record the example of a servant who for some reason had not wisely
invested his master's money and as a result, had no profit to report. In
both cases, the unfaithful servant fell into immediate disfavor with the
master. The fact that Jesus would teach two similar stories within the
period of about a week, so close to his crucifixion, only serves to
emphasize how important he thought the principles of these parables
were.

When the Bible speaks of stewardship, it is really emphasizing an
important aspect and implication of the Lordship of Christ over every
area of the Christian's life. Unfortunately, the spirit of the average Christian today is probably represented best by the citizens who declared, "We
do not want this man to reign over us" (Luke 19:14). Such an attitude in
the Christian life not only robs us of great spiritual blessing, it puts us in
disfavor with God (Luke 19:27). Such an attitude is completely foreign
to the New Testament ideal in which Jesus was viewed as a king (Acts
17:7) and Christians confessed themselves to be His servants (James 1:1).

STEWARDSHIP IS RESPONSIBILITY

The parable of the pounds teaches that everyone has a responsibility to God, even when we have only a little that is committed to us. The Greek word *tuna* translated "pound" in this parable refers to a sum of one hundred denarii worth about $16 total. In terms of the economy of that day, it was worth almost a third of the annual wage of the common laborer. In a culture of extreme wealth and extreme poverty, one *mna* would probably not have impressed the major traders and bankers of the day. Even though the amount was not significant, the servants were each responsible to their master and ultimately accountable for what they did with his resources.

The concern of God is not how much we have, nor necessarily how effective we are with what we have. God is primarily concerned with our faithfulness to the responsibility. Even though different servants produced differently the Lord was pleased with the degree of success each had experienced. His great disappointment was not how little a person produced. He was disappointed with the person who did nothing at all with the pound he had received. The master expected him to use that pound in an effective way just as God wants us to maximize our effective use of the various resources He has entrusted to our stewardship. Responsibility leads to accountability and we will someday each be accountable for our stewardship.

The King is coming back. In the parable of the pounds, the master was pictured as one who would return. The master had no apparent correspondence with his servants while he was away. He did not ask for regular reports, such as a weekly Friday report that expected a Monday response. There seemed to be no communication at all. The workers had their instructions and their responsibility. While there was no weekly evaluation by the boss, the day finally arrived when the master did return and an accountability report was required.

The worker who took his pound and hid it in the ground may have been thinking, "The boss is not coming back." As time wore on, perhaps the servant assumed the rebellious citizens would successfully oppose his master and kill him. Some of the commentaries suggest that the money was hidden in the ground so that the landowner would not have access to it. If the master did not come back, then it would be the worker's. If the worker deposited it in the bank or with traders, it would have been in the master's name If the master never returned, he could not get it back. But if the money was in the ground and the master did not return, it would belong to the servant and him only.

The foundation of stewardship is that we will give an account when the Lord returns and asks for it. Jesus said, "If I go away, I will come again" (John 14:2). When Jesus Christ comes back, we will be accountable for the gifts He has given us. We will not be accountable for someone else's gifts, nor for what others have given to us. We will only be responsible for what God has given to us.

The master trusts us with gifts. Because the master trusts us, he gives us his possessions. The servants were told, "Occupy till I come" (Luke 19:13). The Greek verb *pragmateuornai* translated "occupy" is a commercial term meaning trade. Clearly the master intended his servants to use those pounds as investment tools to increase the master's holdings. Though we are sinners and though we are not perfect, God has entrusted us with gifts and holds us responsible to invest them.

The work of the kingdom is so great that many wonder why God left it to human beings. If most of us had an important task, we probably would not give it to another person, we would do it ourselves. But God has given us the most important task in the world. He has commanded us to evangelize the lost, educate the saints, advance His church and be salt, "a godly influence", on society. Even though this is a great task, He is not going to do it by Himself. God wants to work through us and with us, and in the final analysis, He wants us to fulfill the task for Him. We would not trust other people with a task so awesome. But God who is omnipotent (all powerful) has limited His sovereign power to work through humans like us.

One of the hardest concepts to fathom is the fact that God in His sovereignty has chosen to use people like us to insure the success of His work on earth. What is even more astounding is the realization that the success of His work on earth is to some degree related to our faithfulness in using the resources God has placed at our disposal. We are the channels of God's power in this world.

We are responsible for the light that we have. We must be good stewards of wisdom and knowledge. What we know, we must act upon. But also, we are responsible for the light that we *could* have had. If we do not learn and apply ourselves, we miss the truth of God that we should have learned. That which we miss will be our responsibility.

When we begin to understand this self-limitation of God in entrusting us with resources to do His work, it is natural to become overwhelmed with a tremendous sense of responsibility. Stewardship is acting responsibly with God's resources that are under our authority. Someone has explained it this way: "Responsibility is our response and God's ability." If we forget that GOD IS ABLE even when He has so limited Himself, we will easily become discouraged as we consider all that needs to be done. But God's ability will not become evident until we respond.

We are all judged by how we use our gifts. When the master returned he only had one question, "What have you done with what I gave you?" Although he, like most businessmen, was concerned with the bottom line on the profit and loss statement, he did not outwardly appear upset with the amount of return. He was primarily concerned with how well people used what was given them. The greatest judgment was for the one who did not do anything with what was given to him. Although the Scriptures are silent on the matter, the Lord might have been more pleased with the person who invested his talent and lost all, than with the one who did nothing. When we try our best and lose, we have at least attempted to do something for the Lord. However, in God's kingdom we cannot lose what God has given if we are faithful. Because God works in us and with us, it is impossible to use a gift that God has given to us and not to have a good return with it. Outwardly we may fail, but the day of reckoning is God's, not ours.

In God's kingdom He gives us more responsibility when we demonstrate our faithfulness. When we do our work faithfully, He rewards us with greater responsibility. This is contrary to human nature. Today, when a man has worked faithfully, the boss may send him to Hawaii or some resort for a vacation. But God would give him the increased responsibility of reigning over Hawaii. Because the worker had faithfully produced ten pounds, he was given ten kingdoms to rule.

God gives us more when we do more, because those of us who are faithful want to do more and have proved ourselves responsible. God is not asking us to do something extra that we hate to do or can not do. Instead of saying, "Take a break," God increases our responsibilities.

IRRESPONSIBLE STEWARDSHIP (Luke 19:20-23)

Although the master had entrusted his riches to servants he thought were capable and qualified for the task, at least one of them failed to live up to his expectations. Why did this servant fail to get a good return on the funds left in his trust by the master? As one examines the parable, at least two reasons suggest themselves.

A wrong concept of gifts. The servant who wrapped his gift in a napkin had the wrong concept about the gift of God. He probably felt the gift was his to keep. Maybe he felt he was to give back to the Lord what was given to him. Perhaps he did not want to lost the gift, but just to keep it for God. Whatever his motive, he had a wrong concept of gifts. God wants us to use our gifts, not just admire or hoard them. When the master returns he does not expect us to give only one gift back to Him. He expects more. He expects a return on his investment.

A wrong concept about God. The man who hid his pound was "afraid" of the Master. He said to the Lord, "Thou art an austere man" (19-21). He saw his master as an exacting Lord. In essence, the worker was saying, "Master, I know that you would punish me for losing what you gave-me." He viewed the master only as a judge or vindictive employer.

The master responded in essence saying, "With your own word, I will judge you. Since you expect me to be an 'exacting man', I will judge you an eye for an eye and a tooth for a tooth." (compare 19:22). The master expected his servant to be exacting with the master's resources. He expected the servant to invest them for a dividend.

Rather than viewing God as an *exacting* master, we should recognize Him as an *expecting* master. When people believe in us, they have high expectations for us. When people look to us, they want us to live by those expectations.

God is an expecting Lord. He expects something out of us. Sometimes we act as if we feel God does not expect anything from us, so we attempt little for God and ultimately accomplish little for God. If you expected something from someone and did not get it, not only were you disappointed, you were probably angry. God expects His workers to take the gift and bring back more.

A pastor's wife used to pray for her son reflecting great expectations of him. She would pray, "Lord, I know that you are able to help John not to yield to temptation." The son testified that many times he resisted temptations because his mother expected so much of him. When people expect a lot out of us, first we try harder. Because they believe in us, we want to please them. Secondly, we draw closer to them. We get our strength from the person who believes in us. Because our mothers believed in us, we've drawn closer to them than most other people. We get strength from them. Thirdly, we rise higher because someone believes in us. We achieve more than we could have with our own talents simply because we have been motivated by trust.

The reason some people fail to seek a return on the resources God has placed at their disposal is because of their wrong attitude of God. The see Him only as an austere man or exacting master rather than the expecting master that He is with high expectations for each of our lives. As we understand this attitude of God, we will want to strive to be everything God wants us to become.

THREE ATTITUDES PEOPLE HAVE IN RELATION TO TALENTS

The attitudes reflected by the individuals in these two parables are characteristic of attitudes common in the world and our churches today. If we are going to be responsible with the resources God has placed at our disposal, it is important that we understand these attitudes as we evaluate our own attitudes toward stewardship.

What's God's is mine and I am going to take it. If we have this attitude, we want the possessions of the Lord, the blessings of the Lord, and the resources of the Lord; but we don't want God to reign over us (19:14). We want life on our own terms. Sometimes we are aggressive in this attitude. We "grab all the gusto we can get". We try to live by our own rules.

This attitude will make us "grabbers". It is a worldly attitude. Because the world wants the latest things, they respect the people who have things. However, in the carnal appetite of possessing things, they are never satisfied. People in this category will never have enough of anything.

Sometimes we feel if we could just become a millionaire, we would be happy. Or if we could get a better car, we would be happy; but we never have enough. Bertrand Russell said, "The greatest conflict within mankind is the conflict that wells within him when he realizes he doesn't have as much as he wants."

In a recent poll of one hundred top executives earning $100,000 or more annually, the question was asked, "What is your greatest fear?" By far their response was that in times of inflation they would not have enough money.

If we have the attitude that what is God's is mine, whatever else I can get is mine, we will never be satisfied because we have lived for ourselves.

What's mine is mine and I am going to keep it. With this attitude, we would not steal from God. We would not want to take from others. We would just want what we felt was ours.

We would not be a consumer. We would not be involved in the life process, but be a saver. This attitude would cause us to see life as a picnic in the park where we sit on the benches and enjoy ourselves. We play in the park and take a nap under the trees. We would not consider the park ours. After lunch we pick up our baskets and walk away. We have the attitude, "See, I am not taking from anyone else. I have taken just what is mine."

We will not be guilty of taking away or destroying anything, but we also will not be involved in building or developing anything with His resources either. We fail to recognize that we benefit to some degree from the long-term investment of others and in that sense have the responsibility to consider the needs of future generations.

Those of us who have this attitude never ask, "Who plants the trees, who built the picnic tables, and who maintains the rest rooms?" We do not contribute, nor are we a part of the process of life. We forget that our responsibility is to leave life better for the next generation than we found it We forget that there will be a time when the tree dies, the flower fades and the picnic table decays.

We sit smugly with our picnic basket, saying, "What I have kept is mine."

What's mine is God's and He can have it When we have this attitude, we realize that everything we have belongs to God. We know God will get it whether we give it or not. We realize that we are trustees of what God has given us. We understand the stewardship of God. We become givers of life. We are not takers, nor are we selfish.

In the parable of the Good Samaritan, these three attitudes are apparent (Luke 10:30-37). The first was the thief --"What's his is mine and I'll take it" (10:30). The priest and Levite had the attitude -- "What's mine is mine and I'll keep it" (10:31, 32). They walked by on the other side of the road. The Good Samaritan had the third attitude -- "What's mine is his and I will give it to him" (10:33-35) Lest we should wonder which of these attitudes to adopt personally, Jesus, speaking of the Good Samaritan concluded, "Go, and do thou likewise" (10:37).

CONCLUSION

A man moved to New England and was building a house. He didn't know where to dig his well so he allowed an old timer to find water with a divining stick. (The stick seems to bend where there is an underground river running near the surface.) The old timer said to the new resident, "You must pump the water each day." As he left, he again warned the new resident, "Pump the water each day." At the beginning the new resident pumped water from the well each day and found that the water in the well got sweeter. The more water he pumped, the more water there seemed to be.

After a period of time, the new owner forgot about pumping the well and went on a trip. When he came back there was still water in the well. However, it only lasted two days and then the well went dry. The next time he went to town, he told the old timer about his dry well.

"Did you pump the water every day?" the old timer asked. He explained that an underground river is fed by thousands of capillaries. As water flows through the capillaries, the power of the river keeps them open. But when water is not pumped out of the well, the river becomes stagnant and capillaries fill up, resulting in the river seeking another route through the underground. "You lost the river," the old timer explained, "because you quit using the water."

In the same way, Christians must take from God. The more we claim from God, the more He will give in return. Our wealth is like the water in an underground river; the more we pump our wealth into the work of God, the more God replenishes it for His service. We must pump our wealth continually into the work of God for His increase.

Some Christians lament the fact that something is missing in the spiritual realm. It seems that the joy and enthusiasm that was once part of serving Jesus is gone and the Christian life has almost become an endurance test. When we fail to use the resources God has given us, our spiritual wells will dry up.

We don't need more spiritual food in the Christian community today. We do, however, need more exercise. We need to remember that someday the King is coming back, and when He comes, He is going to ask one question, "What have you done with what I gave you?"

CHAPTER THREE

STEWARDSHIP IS PRIORITIES

BIBLE IN FOCUS: "But seek ye first the kingdom of God, and His righteousness; and all these things shall be added unto you." (Matthew 6:33)

LESSON SCRIPTURE:

That thou appear not unto men to fast, but unto thy Father who is in secret: and thy Father, which seeth in secret, shall reward thee openly.

Lay not up for yourselves treasures upon earth, where moth and rust doth corrupt, and where thieves break through and steal:

But lay up for yourselves treasures in heaven, where neither moth nor rust doth corrupt, and where thieves do not break through nor steal;

For where your treasure is, there will your heart be also.

The lamp of the body is the eye: if therefore thine eye be single, thy whole body shall be full of light.

But if thine eye be evil, thy whole body shall be full of darkness. If therefore the light that is in thee be darkness, how great is that darkness!

No man can serve two masters: for either he will hate the one, and love the other; or else he will hold to the one, and despise the other. Ye cannot serve God and mammon.

Therefore I say unto you, Take no thought for your life, what ye shall eat, or what ye shall drink; nor yet for your body, what ye shall put on. Is not the life more than meat, and the body than raiment?

Behold the fowls of the air: for they sow not, neither do they reap, nor gather into barns; yet your heavenly Father feedeth them. Are ye not much better than they?

Which of you by taking thought can add one cubit unto his stature?

And why take ye thought for raiment? Consider the lilies of the field how they grow; they toil not, neither do they spin.'

And yet I say unto you, that even Solomon in all his glory was not arrayed like one of these.

Wherefore, if God so clothed the grass of the field which today is, and tomorrow is cast into the oven, shall he not much more clothe you, 0 ye of little faith?

Therefore take no thought, saying, What shall we eat? or, What shall we drink? or, Wherewithal shall we be clothed?

(For after all these things do the Gentiles seek:) For your heavenly Father knoweth that ye have need of all these things.

But seek ye first the kingdom of God, and his righteousness; and all these things shall be added unto you.

Take therefore no thought about tomorrow: for the morrow shall take thought for the things of itself. Sufficient unto the day is the evil thereof.

Matthew 6:18-34

INTRODUCTION

There are three things governing the success of our lives. These three things are far more important than money. In many respects, these three things actually govern our use or abuse of our financial resources.

First, our attitude in life determines our altitude in life. If we have the fight view of ourselves and other people, we will succeed in life. We must also have the right attitude about material things and our purpose in life. It is not wrong to possess riches and the symbols of wealth so long as they do not possess us. Stewardship is not simply giving money to God out of guilt or with the view of getting money back. We must give with the fight attitude -- love and adoration for God.

Secondly, relationships also determine personal success in life. If we are to have a meaningful life, we must have the ability to get along with friends, relatives, associates and neighbors. We must know how to develop meaningful relationships. Regardless of how smart or how gifted we are, if we do not have the ability to establish relationships, we will not be as successful in life as we otherwise could be. We may give money and even if we become wealthy, we are poor if we do not have the riches of true friends and close families. Relationships are the real measure of the wealth we have. This means that wealth is not measured by a bank balance or a year-end profit and loss statement. Wealth is measured by the richness of our character and that of those who call us their friends. The kind of relationships we have among our friends, relatives, associates and neighbors reveals volumes about our stewardship of the financial resources at our disposal.

Third, personal priorities in life are probably the greatest of these three factors governing personal success in life. When we have priorities, we also have objectives. We know what we want in life based on what we believe is really important (priorities) and set out objectives which we strive to reach. Without priorities, we could work hard all of our lives, but never accomplish much. To be a success in life, we must know what is important and what will give us the greatest return on our investments. Without priorities, work becomes meaningless and life is empty. When we know our priorities and work towards them, we can have meaning and fulfillment in life.

It is good for us to plan a periodic review of our lives and evaluate our situations in light of our stated priorities. The annual stewardship campaign gives us the opportunity to reflect on our priorities. When we give money to God, we must give it with a sense of priorities. When we give money for that which is important to us, we have a sense of fulfillment. But more importantly, when we give money for things that are important to God, we are investing in eternity.

RECOGNIZING OUR PRIORITIES IN LIFE (Matthew 6:19-34)

After one hundred and two years of continuous publication, the *Chicago Daily News* ceased publishing in February, 1978. It had been one of the greatest newspapers in the country. People could not understand why this great institution collapsed. A TV commentator interviewed one of their Pulitzer Prize award-winning journalists and simply asked, "Why?" The journalist responded, "We forgot our purpose." When their priority to news reporting began to be shuffled in the affairs of making money, they lost their purpose of existence and eventually passed out of existence.

Oliver Wendell Holmes once boarded a train and inadvertently misplaced his ticket. When the conductor came down the aisle to collect the ticket, Holmes frantically looked and could not find it. The conductor recognized who he was and said, "Oh, Mr. Holmes, don't worry. When you find your ticket, just give it to me." Holmes responded, "It is not my ticket I'm worried about. I don't know where I'm going."

Many people could say that about their lives. It seems as though they have boarded a train going somewhere, but they are not really sure where that somewhere is. For all they know, that train could be simply changing box cars in the stockyard.

When Jesus called His disciples together for their first staff meeting, one of the issues he addressed specifically was this area of priorities. He summarized the ultimate priority of every Christian when He said, "But seek ye first the kingdom of God, and his righteousness, and all these things shall be added unto you" (Matthew 6:33). In the course of discussing this topic, Jesus suggested several areas needing discernment in order to determine the real priority of one's life.

What am I giving for? (6:18-21) The first question that Jesus asked involves our attitudes toward money. We can seek the security of money or we can seek the security of God. The priority in stewardship is, "seeking first the Kingdom of God".

Two things are implied in this challenge. First, we must know what is important. Someone has noted that we can have *anything* we want in life, even though we may not be able to have *everything* we want. Therefore, we must be sure we are going after what is really important. We must place a priority on the important things of life. Secondly, we must seek what is important. After we have determined what is important, then we must seek it. The Greek verb for seek, *zeteo,* includes both the ideas of coveting earnestly and striving after something. Only when we have that attitude toward the kingdom and righteousness of God can we claim the conditional promise of this verse, "all things shall be added unto you." That means the issues of our lives will fall into place. When we seek what is important, then the things of life will come to us.

There are two kinds of Christians who have a problem with this promise because of seeking to interpret it out of context. The first is the group who claims the "all things" without accepting the challenge of "seeking the kingdom and righteousness of God". When we are in this group, we believe-we can make demands from God even though our lifestyles are so inconsistent as to be an embarrassment to other more mature Christians. Eventually we become frustrated in life because God is not committed to honor a conditional promise when we fail to do our part and meet the conditions.

A second group of Christians who have a problem with this promise are those who satisfy the condition by earnestly coveting and striving after the kingdom and righteousness of God, but then feel guilty when God begins to bless abundantly in other areas of life. When we are in this position, somewhere along the line we begin to define spirituality in terms of a lack of the niceties of life and are unable to enjoy the blessing of God. We need to understand it is not necessarily more "spiritual" to drive a used Volkswagen than a new Buick

"But seek ye first" suggests there are other alternatives. The word "but" indicates there is another option. Jesus realized that some of us will not seek the Kingdom of God, but seek another option to God's plan. Another option is seeking to save money. These are treasures we consider important because we put them away in special places such as a bank, or. an IRA. God gives us an option. We can "lay up for ourselves treasures on earth," or we can seek first God's plan. When we seek earthly treasures there is the possibility of someone breaking in and stealing them. The other option is to "lay up for yourself treasures in Heaven". There, thieves cannot break in, nor can we lose our treasures.

WHAT AM I GIVING FOR? (MATTHEW 6:19-20)			
Option One Treasure On Earth	Subject to Ruin	Subject to Rust	Subject to Robbery
Option Two Treasure In Heaven	Exempt from Ruin	Exempt from Rust	Exempt from Robbery

"Where your treasure is, there will your heart be also" (6:21). Our money reveals our heart. Jesus was saying, "Show me your treasure and I'll show you your heart." Our check stubs or our credit card bill tells what is important to us. Often we try to determine our spirituality by our prayer lives or Bible reading, but our check stubs are a more accurate barometer of what is really important to us.

What am I looking for? (6:22,23) "What am I looking for?" is a question that when answered tells us what it is we will eventually find. Just as a burglar never finds a policeman and boys cutting school never find a teacher, so those of us who refuse to submit to the Lordship of Christ never "find" His blessings. Jesus also asks if we are living for things that will last or things that will slip away. He indicates our sight is imperative regarding money. "The light of the body is the eye; if, therefore, thine eye be single, thy whole body shall be full of light" (6:22). Our priorities are evident in the focus of our lives. If we have the correct view of what is really important in life, everything else falls into order. "But if thine eye be evil, thy whole body shall be filled full of darkness" (6:23).

What am I living for?" (6:24) Jesus said it is impossible to serve two masters. It is impossible to serve God's kingdom and the world's kingdoms. When we try to serve two masters, we will be stretched, divided and absolutely miserable. People can tell what we live for by who we serve.

In order to make ends meet today, many people try working two jobs for two different companies. Some people have been successful in moon-lighting by carefully planning their employment and life into a precise timetable. But no matter how hard we try, we Christians are not able to moonlight by serving God on one shift and wealth on another. But that is not the kind of service God or mammon (money) demands. The Greek word used in verse 24 is not *latreuo* which means to work or serve for hire, but rather *douleuo* meaning to serve as a slave or one who is in bondage to another. This is the kind of service expected by both God and mammon and it is impossible to have that kind of committed service to two masters. Even though we might try for a while, the crisis will eventually come when we must decide if we prefer to be in bondage to God or endure financial bondage.

What am I dying for? (6:25-32) Dwight L. Moody once declared, "A man has not found something worth living for until he has found some-thing worth dying for." Jesus emphasized this truth when he spoke of the stressful lifestyles characteristic of those with wrong priorities in life. Par-ticularly, Jesus identified anxiety/stress over such things as life, food, drink, clothing and unchangeable physical features like height as more characteristic of a non-Christian approach to life.

Jesus was not instructing us not to plan ahead when he said, "take no thought for your life..." (6:25). Had he meant to imply this, He would have used the verb m*elo* which implies the care of forethought and inter-est, but not anxiety. He did use this word once describing a shortcoming of the hireling who did not "care" for the sheep (John 10:13). By impli-cation, He seems to imply in that context it is right to have a proper concern over some things, a caring or concern characterized by careful forethought and genuine interest. The verb used in Matthew 6, however, is *merimnao* meaning a care of anxiety or a distracting care. This caring or "taking thought of" is the kind of anxious concern which distracts from other important concerns and hinders one from getting things accomplished.

God has created man physically to be able to handle a certain amount of stress which is actually healthy, but a stress overload can actually kill us The healthy limit of stress is the concerns of each day as they become apparent. As one man once noted, "I have had many problems that troubled me in life, but most of them never happened." We would do well to heed Jesus' advice even if only for our health's sake, "Take therefore no thought for the morrow: for the morrow shall take thought for the things of itself. Sufficient unto the day is its own evil" (6:34).

When we are anxious over money, we will eventually die for money. If on the other hand, we live for God's kingdom and righteousness, that becomes the object of our sacrifice. Just as a missionary might have to sacrifice his life as a martyr to take the gospel to a primitive unreached tribe, so God wants us to be a "living sacrifice" which is often much harder. One man learned this truth when he recited a love poem to his wife and concluded the poem with the thought that his love for her was so great he would even lay down his life for her. "Oh," his wife sighed. "But will you wash the dishes for me?"

What are you longing for? (6:32,33) Ultimately, the priority of life is evident in the secret longings and deep-seated desires of the heart. For some it is a new Mercedes or luxury automobile. Others long for a house on the beach or back in the mountains. Still others want more than anything else to see their name on the company letterhead as the company president. What is it we are really longing for? That is our real priority in life.

As noted above, the word *seek* implies the idea of coveting earnestly and striving after. It is not wrong to have such longings if our desires are governed by the right priority. There is a difference between the things the Gentiles or people of this world long after and that which the Christian should have as his deep-seated desire. And when Jesus tells us to seek God's kingdom and righteousness, He does not mean we should do it for a weekend, month or even a year. This verb is not an aorist tense verb which would imply seeking once and for all but a tense emphasizing a continuous unending exercise of seeking. Just as the people of the world are constantly seeking after the transient material things of this world, so we as Christians need to be constantly seeking after the reality of God's kingdom and righteousness.

MAKING PRIORITY DECISIONS

We make priority judgments every day of our lives. We make value decisions about everything. We need to seek things that are consistent with our priorities in life which is God's kingdom and righteousness.

The above questions reveal the priority of the decisions we make in life. Some of us become mystical when we talk about seeking God. When we do, we show our lack of knowledge and understanding about it. We seem to arrive at decisions totally unrelated to the real issues of life. But seeking God is not some mystical discipline of the Dark Ages. It is practical, measurable, and obtainable.

There are three questions that we need to ask concerning the priority decisions in our lives. Answering these questions can help insure that our major decisions in life are consistent with our predetermined priority of seeking the kingdom and righteousness of God.

Will it last? (6:19,20) When we make decisions, many of them have eternal consequences. Therefore, we should make decisions with the long-range viewpoint.

Jesus described two kinds of people. The first put their value on this earth and the other put their value in Heaven. If we are in the group who puts value on this earth, we store things up while those of us who put the most value in the eternal perspective realize that things will last for eternity only if invested in Heaven. "Is not the life more than meat, and the body more than raiment?" (6:25) Therefore, before making major decisions, we should ask ourselves the question, "What type of lasting value will this decision give to my family? to my church? to me?"

Will it bring light? (6:22,23) This question asks if it helps. Will it elevate people? Is it positive? Does it make me a better person? Does it make my family better? We should always ask if a decision has a positive sense and if it will help guide in the way of righteousness. Most of our major decisions in life will have an impact on the lives of others. To the best of our ability, we should make the kind of decisions that have a positive impact rather than a destructive influence. It should follow the guidelines of Matthew 5:16, "Let your light so shine before men, that they may see your good works, and glorify your Father which is in Heaven."

Is it of faith? (6:39) We should also ask if the decision is made in faith, i.e. not faith in ourselves, but faith in God. Jesus described His listeners, "Oh ye of little faith" (6:30) The phrase "little faith" was used by Jesus to describe His disciples characterized by a mixture of both faith and doubt. These people were making their decisions outside of faith. While they trusted God to save them for all eternity, they tended to doubt God was able to supply their basic needs. The Bible teaches God is able both to save our souls for eternity (Hebrews 7:25) and supply our needs here and now (Philippians 4:19). If God takes care of the birds and the lilies, He can and will take care of us.

We should make all decisions underneath the umbrella of God's provision for us. this does not mean that God will feed the lazy. But underneath the umbrella there are both privileges and responsibilities. When we meet the conditions of God's conditional promises, only then can we claim God's promises. Then God will take care of us.

Some carnal Christians have messed up their lives by claiming promises without meeting the conditions required. They complain that God has not taken care of them, yet they have not sought God's kingdom first. God will not bless us if we have not worked, learned and obeyed the principles of Scripture when we have had an opportunity to do so.

HOW JESUS MADE DECISIONS

Our personal success in our Christian lives over the next twelve months will be governed by our willingness to seek God first. The consequences we suffer today are a result of the decisions we made yesterday. And the decisions we make today will determine our happiness tomorrow. Notice how Jesus made life-changing decisions.

Jesus chose. The key word in making decisions is to choose. We are not what we are today by accident. We are the sum total of all the decisions we have made in our lives, plus those times we did not make decisions. When we choose not to choose, we at least ought to know that we chose not to choose. We may throw up our hands as though we can't make a decision. Yet we live by the results of our "non-decision". We have arrived at where we are in life by decisions and non-decisions, and we are responsible for both. Therefore, it only makes sense to be like Jesus and control our lives and destinies by choosing to choose.

Jesus withdrew. When we make spiritual decisions, we have to withdraw from the world's system, so we will not make worldly decisions. To make spiritual decisions, we must let God and not the world influence us.

Jesus had to withdraw from the world so he could spend time in prayer. He had to go alone so he could think His way through decisions. He went into the wilderness for forty days before beginning His ministry. He prayed all night before choosing the twelve apostles. He spent time alone in prayer before every major decision or circumstance in His life and ministry on earth. What Jesus did is no different than what we also must do if we are going to make the right priority decisions in life.

If we do not withdraw from the world's system, it will adversely influence us to make the wrong decisions. Jesus not only withdrew from Satan and worldly influences, at times He withdrew from those He loved the most -- His disciples. Sometimes those who love us most will influence us apart from what is best for us. We cannot allow people to put us into a mold that is not spiritual. When making major decisions, we may need to get alone (1) to pray, (2) to think through issues, (3) to clear the mind of inconsequential data, (4) to gain a godly perspective, and (5) to understand how to best apply biblical principles to the particular situation and decisions we must make. This is the way to make good decisions.

Jesus prayed. If Jesus who was God felt it necessary to spend time in prayer, how can we do otherwise? The urgency of His decision compelled Him to pray. How much more should earthly people spend time in prayer, for we do not have the perfection that Jesus had. As we make decisions, we should first of all ask God for the wisdom from above that only He can give (James 1:5). When confronted with a major decision, it may be wise to accompany our prayer for wisdom with a period of fasting (Isaiah 58:8,9).

He obeyed Jesus made all decisions in keeping with the Word of God. Jesus said, "My meat is to do the will of Him that sent me" (John 4:34). By this He meant His food was to obey the Father. A good decision had to be in keeping with the will of God, which is found in the Word of God. As He made decisions in life, He did so with an underlying commitment to obey the directives of His Father.

We should not have to choose whether or not we will obey the directives and guidance of God in making a particular decision. That should already be settled. We should have the attitude that we will always do right. We do not choose to obey God as He reveals His will. We have already made that decision. We live by the principle that we will obey God in making every decision. We don't have to think about the moral ramifications of drunkenness or backsliding when looking at the choice of drinking alcoholic beverages. We have already made a choice to simply obey God. We need to study the Scriptures and seek God in prayer to discern His will, but we do not have to pray about doing what we already know God wants us to do.

Jesus declared. He knew any and every decision needed to be declared. He was willing to tell others what He had decided. Sometimes this step will make us popular with others who like the consequences of our decisions. At other times we will encounter opposition and criticism when we inform others of an unpopular decision. Regardless of the anticipated consequences, we need to declare our decisions. When we make proper priority decisions in life, we can declare those decisions knowing that regardless of the immediate consequences, ultimately our decisions will prove to have been the best course of action.

CONCLUSION

Some Christians have developed an erroneous view of the Christian life that views Christ as a kind of sanctified Santa Claus. They believe they can childishly sit back and make demands from God without accepting personal responsibility or even having right priorities in life. Perhaps we forget that according to Dutch legend, the jolly red-suited fat man also left lumps of coal in the wooden shoes of boys and girls who had not obeyed their parents in the preceding year.

We have no legitimate right to claim a promise from God until we have done our parts in meeting the conditions associated with the particular promises. We are not to come to God seeking all the things Gentiles seek after, but rather seeking God's kingdom and righteousness. Jesus modeled this principle when He humbled Himself and left the glory that was rightfully His to become a man and provide for our salvation. Because Jesus sought first God's kingdom and righteousness, God rewarded Him by restoring Him to His original glory and greatly elevating His name. The Apostle Paul points out that ought also to be the characteristic attitude of the believer.

Christmas is nothing more than Jesus who was everything becoming nothing so that we who are nothing can become everything. Yet some Christians today believe it is requiring too much to expect them to give up some minor luxury for the sake of the kingdom of God. When we settle the priority issue in life, we will adopt the attitude of Christ concerning stewardship. Only then will we understand the wisdom of Jim Elliott who as a college student penned the words, "He is no fool who gives what he cannot keep to gain what he cannot lose."

CHAPTER FOUR

STEWARDSHIP IS GIVING

BIBLE IN FOCUS: "Give, and it shall be given unto you; good measure, pressed down, and shaken together, and running over, shall men give into your bosom. For with the same measure that ye mete withal it shall be measured to you again." Luke 6:38

LESSON SCRIPTURE:

But I say unto you that hear, Love your enemies, do good to them which hate you.

Bless them that curse you, and pray for them which despitefully use you.

And unto him that smiteth thee on the one cheek offer also the other; and him that taketh away thy cloak forbid not to take thy coat also.

Give to every man that asketh of thee; and of him that taketh away thy goods ask them not again.

And as ye would that men should do to you, do ye also to them likewise.

For if ye love them who love you, what thank have ye? For sinners also love those who love them.

And if ye do good to them which do good to you, what thank have ye? For sinners also do even the same.

And if ye lend to them of whom ye hope to receive, what thank have ye? For sinners also lend to sinners, to receive as much again.

But love your enemies, and do good, and lend, hoping for nothing again,' and your reward shall be great, and ye shall be the children of the Highest: for he is kind unto the unthankful and to the evil

Be ye therefore merciful, as your Father also is merciful

Judge not, and ye shall not be judged: condemn not, and ye shall not be condemned: forgive, and ye shall be forgiven.

Give, and it shall be given unto you; good measure, pressed down, and shaken together, and running over, shall men give into your bosom. For with the same measure that ye mete withal it shall be measured to you again.

Luke 6:27-38

INTRODUCTION

Love is the foundation for stewardship. As someone has well noted, "You can give without loving, but you cannot love without giving." Love is the motivation for everything we do, and this is particularly so in our stewardship.

One of the best known verses in Scripture teaches us that God loved us and gave to us. "For God so *loved* the world that He *gave...*" (John 3:16). You cannot separate loving and giving, because true love always leads to giving. The object of your love knows no limitations, or constraints. The young man who loves his girl friend never thinks that he gives enough to her. The mother who loves her baby would give anything for it. The one who truly loves God knows no limits in giving to Him.

When the Scriptures describe the love which motivates the believers in our service for Christ, it often uses the Greek term *agape*. This term has been called "the characteristic word of Christianity" because it is so often used in the Scriptures to describe both the motive and expression of Christian service. While there are many Greek words translated "love" in the English Bible, and each of these expresses different kinds of love, *agape* love can be defined only in terms of the act of giving. It is a love that has God as its primary object and is not necessarily related to an impulse of the emotions. In fact, *agape* love is most often pictured in Scripture as voluntarily taking a course of action contrary to what the natural feelings would appear to dictate.

A little girl took all of the money out of her bank, stuffed it into her purse and went to the store. She told her father, "I want to spend all my money on mother." The father asked, "Why?" "Because I love her so much," came the reply.

People think that if a person is a millionaire, he will give much to God. Experience suggests that is probably not true. Giving has nothing to do with our financial state; it has everything to do with our love relationship to God. Those who love God the most make the greatest sacrifice for Him. This does not necessarily mean they give the largest monetary gift to God although that is often the case. Giving is not measured by the amount of money given, but is measured by the sacrifice made for the purpose of giving. The widow who gave only two mites made the greatest sacrifice, because it was all she had.

THE CHARACTER OF CHRISTIAN GIVING (Luke 6:27-38)

Because love is characteristic of God in His very nature, it is expected that the same kind of love should be a part of the Christian's regenerated character. The Apostle John twice reminded his readers that love was characteristic of God and on both occasions he made specific application to the love life of the believer. First, he argued a person who does not love really does not have a personal relationship with God. "He that loveth not, knoweth not God; for God is love" (I John 4:8). Later in the same chapter, he restated this truth in more positive terms. "And we have known and believed the love that God hath to us. God is love, and he that dwelleth in love dwelleth in God, and God in him" (I John 4:16). If we affirm God is a God of love, we must also acknowledge that characteristic attribute must also be evident in our lives as believers.

There is, therefore, a world of difference between Christian giving and that of the world. Christian giving is an expression and evidence of the indwelling love of God. In the passage under consideration in this chapter, notice the nine times the verbs "loving" or "giving" are used. Six times Jesus speaks of loving and three times uses the verb giving. It is as though He is emphasizing the truth that love is the beginning and ending of all Christian giving. The following are characteristics of Christian giving.

Christian giving returns good for evil (6:27-30). We Christians should return good for the evil we receive. The world says, "an eye for the eye", but as Christians, we take the shirts off of our backs to give to others. We love our enemies and pray for those who mistreat us.

When a little baby is born into the world, he is nothing but a consumer. He demands his rights, cries for attention and wants his needs met immediately. Yet we fall in love with that little baby and give everything we can to him. It is because the baby belongs to us; it is natural to love him.

However, it is unnatural to love our enemies. How can we love them? There are two kinds of love -- love of the heart and love of the will. When the Bible speaks of the love of the heart, it uses the Greek word *philanthropia* which literally means "a brotherly love for mankind". Most often this word is translated "kindness" in Scripture. While that is part of Christian love, Christian love goes beyond heart-felt kindness and also includes the self-sacrificing *agape* love of the will. It is not natural to love an enemy out of our hearts. Even as Christians we find it difficult to turn our hearts toward our enemies who want to hurt us. A Christian's love for an enemy must come from our wills.

God is the model for loving our enemies. "While we were yet sinners, Christ died for us" (Romans 5:8). When we love our enemies like the Father, we initiate good for evil. When we are abused by others, Jesus advises "killing them with kindness".

Former American President Abraham Lincoln in many ways personified this aspect of Christian giving. He was often criticized for his positive treatment of his sworn enemies. One of Lincoln's enemies once stated in print he thought Lincoln was a mistake and the American public would live to regret placing such an obvious incompetent in the White House. The nature of the critic's attack on Lincoln even degenerated to the place where Lincoln's physical features were compared to those of a gorilla and the ape came out on top. Later, when war broke out between the States, Lincoln asked that critic to serve as his Secretary of War.

Lincoln's advisers were appalled with the President's actions. When they asked him why he would choose his critic for such an important post, he responded he thought Staunton was the best man for the job. When they advised him that he should seek to destroy his enemies rather than treat them like friends, he reminded them he was destroying his enemies-when he made them his friends. Later, when Lincoln died, Staunton was standing by the President's bedside. As he watched Lincoln breathe his last breath, he uttered the words, "There dies the greatest ruler of mankind the world has ever seen."

A godly pastor had two boys who were aggressive in their play. They climbed on the neighbor's garage and ran through her hedge. They were not mean, just typical boys. The neighbor came and complained to the godly pastor who said to his wife, "Bake an extra pie." Then he took the pie over and apologized for the boys. This happened each time the boys overstepped their boundary. In the process of time the lady came to love the pastor, his wife and eventually even the boys. The love that didn't automatically come from the heart, grew in the will. It is difficult for us to love those who are suing us and those who mistreat us. But we can pray for grace and strength to love those people.

We will show our spiritual maturity by how we respond to those who have treated us wrongfully. It does not take spiritual maturity to treat others well who treat us well. Even the unsaved do that. Our ability to take adversity in a Christian spirit and to return good for evil does take spiritual maturity.

Christian giving elevates society (Luke 6:31). When we give, society becomes a better place. Whether we are giving for foreign missions, preaching the gospel, or teaching the Word of God, the influence of Christianity makes the world a better place.

We should treat others as we want them to treat us. The Golden Rule is found in some form in every religion of the world. A Jewish Rabbi, Hillel, said, "What is hateful to thee, do not to another." An Alexandrian philosopher said, "What you hate to suffer, do not do to anyone else." Socrates said, "What things make you angry when you suffer them at the hands of others, do not do to those other people." The stoics declared, "What you do not wish to be done to yourself do not do to anyone else." Confucius said, "What you do not want done to yourself, do not do to others." The worldly statement of the Golden Rule is negative --"don't do to others what would be uncomfortable to us." But the Christian adds the positive, "Do to others what you want done to you" (compare Luke 6:31), which is God's standard. God wants us to do positive things, not just refrain from negative things. We can refrain from the negative, but that does not make us God-like. It is a lot easier not to do what we don't want to do, than it is to do what we don't want to do. The Golden Rule as taught by Jesus is the healer of wrong relationships.

What do we want other people to do for us? What are some of the positive things we want them to do to us?

(1) *We want people to give us the benefit of the doubt.* We do not want others to judge us without knowing all of the facts. How often have we been hurt or misunderstood because someone else did not get the facts or misinterpreted our motives? At those times we normally wish we could somehow get the benefit of the doubt so as to explain our good intentions.

(2) *We want people to give us another opportunity to do better.* Many people say, "You will never do that to me again," which means they will not give us another chance. None of us is perfect. We know that, but how often do we forget that when we see someone else fail and in the process hurt us personally? We and they want to do better and be given the opportunity to improve.

(3) *We want people to admit that they make mistakes.* We are not looking to humiliate them, we only want them to join with us in our human pilgrimage. One of the worst things in life is to talk to someone

who never makes a mistake. It's not that they are arrogant; they just make us uncomfortable and destroy the potential of developing meaningful relationships with them.

Christian giving is more than trading (6:32-35). Christian giving is more than Christmas swapping with God or others. We often buy someone a Christmas gift because we think they are going to buy us a gift. But that is not Christian motivation. The world responds but the Christian gives. The world responds because it is going to get something in return, but the Christian gives because he wants to give. He gives to others because God gives to him.

If we love only those who love us, that is not uniquely Christian. The world does that. The same with giving money. If we give to those who will give to us, that is not Christian. When Jesus said, "expecting nothing in return," (6:35) He was speaking of radical giving. This kind of giving is based on *agape* love. And when our giving is based on love, it is fanatical and radical because it takes the dedication of our whole life.

We should not feel the Bible is commanding only the rich about giving. We cannot place the giving burden only on those who need a tax credit or can give large endowments. In this teaching, Jesus turned His gaze on His disciples and said, "Blessed be ye poor," (6:20) indicating the lesson on giving was for everyone regardless of the amount that could be given.

Jesus used the Greek word *ptochos* rather than *penes* to describe the poverty of His disciples. *Penes* is the poverty of a man who so poor he must work for a living and has nothing superfluous in his lifestyle. *Ptochos* refers to absolute or abject poverty of a man who has nothing at all. It is related to the verb which means to crouch or cower and describes the humiliating kind of poverty that drives a man to cower away from others. Jesus used the same word for poverty when he described the spiritual poverty of his disciples (Matthew 5:3). Therefore, these instructions for giving were given to those who were both poor in spirit, *and* poor in the pocketbook. When Jesus talked to the poor, His subject was giving. Obviously this was not because He wanted or needed their money. He knew they could not give as much as the rich. Jesus talked to the poor about giving because He wanted to enrich their lives.

We may try to use the excuse, "I cannot give to the church because I owe so much." But our bank balance has nothing to do with giving to God. We may say that we must have money for ourselves and our families, therefore we cannot give to God. When we use our families as an excuse for not giving, it is a cop out. More often, the reason for our financial bondage is a failure to discipline our lives. We have not learned that stewardship is management and we are not managing our lives well. Usually the resulting problems first show up in our financial affairs. When we begin applying the sound principles of biblical stewardship to life, we will give to God out of love and learn to discipline our lives. Then we will not only give that proportion which belongs to God, but we will manage the rest of our lives according to the biblical principles. Well managed lives glorify God.

Jesus referred His disciples to the widow who dropped two mites into the temple treasury. He said they ought to give like her. She gave all. It was not measured by how much she gave but by her attitude and obedience.

The rich young ruler wanted to follow Jesus Christ. When Jesus convicted him because of his wealth, the Bible says, "He was very sorrowful" (sad). He was not willing to learn the stewardship of money. The "cares of this world" hindered him from having a meaningful relationship with God.

In the parable of the pounds, a person's stewardship had nothing to do with how many pounds a man had. It had everything to do with his character, faithfulness, and how much he loved his master and expressed that love in good stewardship.

Christian giving is modeled by God (6:35,36). The world invests its money according to that which will give a good return. This is not necessarily based on selfishness or hoarding. It is based on being a good steward of assets and resources. Investment is what banks, mutual funds and IRA's are all about.

God is a good business man and He invests in us. Yet God has invested in a product which at the time of investment must have seemed to have a high risk factor and subsequent low yield. While we were helpless, God loved us (Romans 5:6). While we were sinners, Christ died for us (Romans 5:8). While we were enemies, He reconciled us (Romans 5:10). The investment of God is based on mercy.

The world system is not based on mercy, but on merit. In other words, If you can do something for me (return a good percentage), I will do something for you (loan you my money). Business is run by the merit system. Merit is based on giving value in return for money. But everyone who knows Jesus Christ is a product of the mercy system. We were saved by mercy, not our merit (Ephesians 2:8-9).

Christian giving is an attitude that affects others and ourselves (6:37). When we give money to God, it not only affects ourselves, it also affects others. Do not condemn others, and you will not be condemned. If we forgive others, we too will be forgiven. Jesus described the person who sees a speck in his brother's eye, when he has a log in his own eye (6:41,42). Giving involves an attitude.

It is not our place to measure someone else's spirituality by what we think. If we judge others we will be judged by God. Our standard for judging others will be God's standard for judging us. We will be judged in both accomplishment and attitude. While we may pass God's standard of accomplishment, we will fail God's standard of attitude. We will be judged by our attitudes of either forgiving our brothers or being critical of our brothers. Those of us who are forgiving of others will encounter a very forgiving God. Those of us who are critical and condemning will meet the same spirit when God evaluates our stewardship.

Christian giving brings unexpected blessings from unexpected sources (6:38). Jesus promises, "Give, and it shall be given unto you" (6:38). We will get a blessing back when we give to others. By our standard of measure, it will be measured to us in return.

One person asked his minister, "How much should I give to God?"

"How much do you want in life?" his minister replied. When another person asked his pastor if he should base his proportionate giving on his net or gross income, the wise minister responded with a question, "Do you want a net or gross blessing from God?"

God gives to us based on how we give to Him. We can't out give God because He multiplies our gift in His work and returns to us accordingly. We have little blessings from God when we invest very little with God. We must learn the stewardship of giving.

If we set the level of the blessing we want, we will receive them. God teaches that we can expect blessings, but those blessings usually come from unexpected places. A person to whom we give a coat will not give us another coat down the road. But since everything comes back to us, a blessing will return to us from unexpected sources. God does not always return to us what we give away. When we give away our money, some-one may help us gain a new position with a raise in salary. If we give away our time, someone may help us financially. As we give away our counsel and advice, someone may befriend our children and strengthen their character or outlook on life.

When we become a giver, we will ultimately become a receiver in return. If we are only spiritual consumers, we never become spiritual receivers.

THE SPIRIT OF CHRISTIAN GIVING

There is more to Christian giving than certain characteristic acts which might seem to be otherwise unnatural. Because Christian giving is an expression of the indwelling love of God, there is often a spirit accompanying an act of *agape* love that is "better felt than telt". The open hand that gives to the needs of others is accompanied by an open heart of compassion which is the original motive in giving.

A spiritual lifestyle. Christian giving is more than isolated acts of kindness to those in need -- it is a constant spiritual lifestyle. Giving money to God is not a one-time event, but rather a continual attitude that affects the process of life. Jesus did not talk about going with someone the second mile or giving someone our coats as a one-time act. He was talking about an attitude that becomes a part of our way of life.

Some of us will keep count of our giving with an attitude of quitting when we hit a certain point. Then we quit giving and expect others to take over for us. But Christian giving does not keep score, nor does it keep a balance sheet. We give to God because we love Him. As we grow in our love, we will grow in our giving. And as we grow in giving, we will also grow in our love for God because "where your treasure is, there will your heart be also" (Matthew 6:21).

An expression of grace. It takes grace to be that kind of a consistent giver and that grace can only come from God. Jesus described the giver who gives by grace, not grit. If His disciples had been merely *penes* poor, they may have been able to make some sacrifices, roll up their shirt sleeves, grit their teeth and give to God. But these disciples were *ptochos* poor and therefore could not obey Jesus' command to give even if they wanted to, apart from the grace of God. Have you ever noticed how many of the biblical examples of giving were individuals who gave out of their deep poverty? As we mature in other graces in the Christian life, God wants us also to excel in the grace of giving also (II Corinthians 8:7).

CONCLUSION

Years ago a Sunday School missionary preached in a church hall and made an appeal for funds to help buy books that could be used in starting new Sunday Schools in the American frontier. As others gave money for the cause, one little girl wanted to help reach boys and girls through Sunday Schools, but had not money to give. As the offering plate was passed down her aisle, she slipped her prize possession in life -- her mother's gold wedding band -- off her finger and placed it in the plate.

After the service, a businessman came to the missionary deeply moved by the little girl's sacrifice. He had seen the girl silently place the ring in the offering plate and knew it represented the memory of her recently deceased mother. The man offered to redeem the ring for far more than the ring was worth, if the missionary agreed to return the ring to the orphan girl. But when the missionary tried to return it, she refused, noting she had given it to help purchase books to start Sunday Schools that would reach boys and girls and tell them about Jesus. When she could not be persuaded to take back the ring, the missionary kept it and used it as an object lesson as he represented the cause of the Sunday School mission. Over the years, the missionary re-told the story many times. The little girl's example of sacrifice resulted in raising thousands of dollars needed for the expansion of Sunday Schools.

God wants us to be a blessing and receive a blessing by giving to Him out of our poverty so He can enrich our lives. It is easy to find reasons why we can't afford to give to God, but that only hinders Him in His desire to bless us. When we realize the great resources of the world God has at His disposal, it is obvious God does not want us to give because He needs or wants our money. God wants us to learn the stewardship of giving so that He can be justified in abundantly blessing our lives.